MAN-MADE |
TITANIC

by Jenny Fretland VanVoorst

pogo

Ideas for Parents and Teachers

Pogo Books let children practice reading informational text while introducing them to nonfiction features such as headings, labels, sidebars, maps, and diagrams, as well as a table of contents, glossary, and index.

Carefully leveled text with a strong photo match offers early fluent readers the support they need to succeed.

Before Reading

- "Walk" through the book and point out the various nonfiction features. Ask the student what purpose each feature serves.
- Look at the glossary together. Read and discuss the words.

Read the Book

- Have the child read the book independently.
- Invite him or her to list questions that arise from reading.

After Reading

- Discuss the child's questions. Talk about how he or she might find answers to those questions.
- Prompt the child to think more. Ask: Did you know about the *Titanic* disaster before reading this book? What more do you want to learn after reading it?

Pogo Books are published by Jump!
5357 Penn Avenue South
Minneapolis, MN 55419
www.jumplibrary.com

Library of Congress Cataloging-in-Publication Data

Names: Fretland VanVoorst, Jenny, 1972- author.
Title: Titanic / by Jenny Fretland VanVoorst.
Description: Minneapolis, MN: Jump!, Inc., [2018]
Series: Pogo. Man-made disasters | "Pogo Books are published by Jump!" | Audience: Ages 7-10.
Identifiers: LCCN 2017041140 (print)
LCCN 2017039632 (ebook)
ISBN 9781624967054 (ebook)
ISBN 9781620319222 (hardcover: alk. paper)
ISBN 9781620319239 (pbk.)
Subjects: LCSH: Titanic (Steamship) –Juvenile literature. Shipwrecks–North Atlantic Ocean–History–20th century–Juvenile literature.
Classification: LCC G530.T6 (print)
LCC G530.T6 F74 2018 (ebook) | DDC 910.9163/4–dc23
LC record available at https://lccn.loc.gov/2017041140

Editor: Kristine Spanier
Book Designer: Michelle Sonnek
Photo Researcher: Michelle Sonnek

Photo Credits: axily/Shutterstock, cover (iceberg); Nerthuz/Shutterstock, cover (ship); krtphotoslive793793/Newscom, 1 (ship); Sergey Skleznev/Shutterstock, 1 (buoy); Mulevich/Shutterstock, 3; Titanic Images/Universal Images Group/Agefotostock, 4; Volodymyr Goinyk/Shutterstock, 5 (iceberg); YIUCHEUNG/Shutterstock, 5 (sky); Max Dannenbaum/Getty, 6-7; patrick frilet/Marka/Superstock, 8; David Paul Morris/Stringer/Getty, 9; GL Archive/Alamy, 10-11; Axel Bueckert/Shutterstock, 12-13 (scrapbook); Everett Collection Historical/Alamy, 12-13 (Brown), 14-15; Illustrated London News Ltd/Pantheon/Superstock, 12-13 (Smith); Bettmann/Getty, 12-13 (Guggenheim), 16-17; Alex Alekseev/Shutterstock, 18; UniversalImagesGroup/Getty, 19; Emory Kristof/Getty, 20-21; celebrity/Alamy, 23.

Printed in the United States of America at Corporate Graphics in North Mankato, Minnesota.

TABLE OF CONTENTS

CHAPTER 1
Iceberg! 4

CHAPTER 2
Unsinkable 8

CHAPTER 3
Lessons Learned 18

ACTIVITIES & TOOLS
Try This! 22
Glossary 23
Index 24
To Learn More 24

CHAPTER 1

ICEBERG!

The date was April 14, 1912. Aboard *Titanic*, passengers danced and dined. Some strolled on the deck. Others were asleep in their cabins.

It was a moonless night in the North Atlantic. At 11:40 P.M. a call rang out from the **crow's nest**. "**Iceberg**! Right ahead!"

iceberg

CHAPTER 1

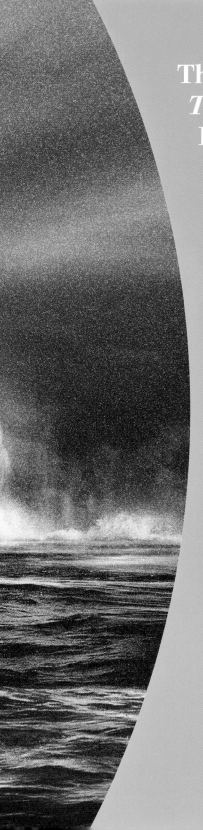

Then came a dull thud. Metal tore. *Titanic* began taking on water. It sank in only three hours. *Titanic* went from a **vessel** full of life to a wreck on the ocean floor. The ship was said to be unsinkable. How could this disaster have happened?

CHAPTER 2

UNSINKABLE

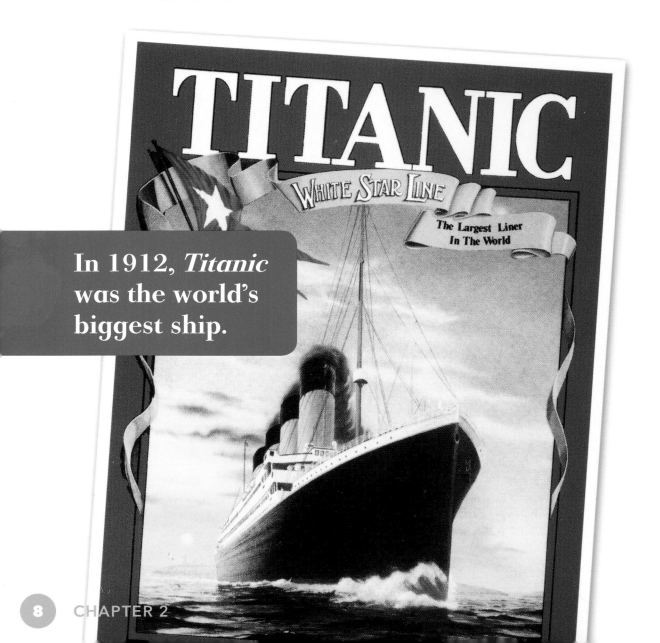

In 1912, *Titanic* was the world's biggest ship.

It was the most comfortable. It was the most **elegant**. It was also thought to be the safest.

Grand Staircase

The **hull** was made up of rooms divided by heavy walls. The walls, called **bulkheads**, had watertight doors. The rooms could be sealed off from each other if one had a leak.

hull

TAKE A LOOK!

Titanic had 15 bulkheads. This created 16 sections. They were not sealed at the top.

■ = *Titanic*　■ = bulkheads

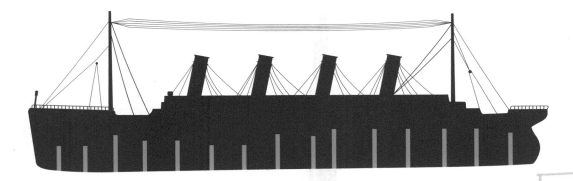

- **Length:** 883 feet (269 meters); nearly the length of three football fields
- **Height:** 175 feet (53 m); about the height of a 17-story building
- **Weight:** 52,000 tons (47,174 tonnes); about the weight of 140 jumbo jets
- **Cost to Build:** $7.5 million; about $400 million in today's dollars

Everyone felt safe on that first trip. The ship was traveling from England to New York Harbor. It carried more than 1,300 passengers. A crew of nearly 900 worked on board. Many wealthy and famous people were on the ship. It also carried many **emigrants**.

Molly Brown, Titanic survivor

Edward John Smith, captain of Titanic

Benjamin Guggenheim, passenger who did not survive

gash

Four days into the trip, a large iceberg was spotted. It was in the ship's path. But *Titanic* was going too fast to avoid it.

To the passengers, the crash just felt like a mild thump. But the crew knew better. The iceberg had ripped a **gash** in the ship's steel hull. Water began pouring in.

The **bow** of the ship pitched downward. Seawater poured from one bulkhead to the next.

The force caused the ship to break in half. By 2:20 A.M. on April 15, the ship's **stern** also sank. More than 1,500 people died.

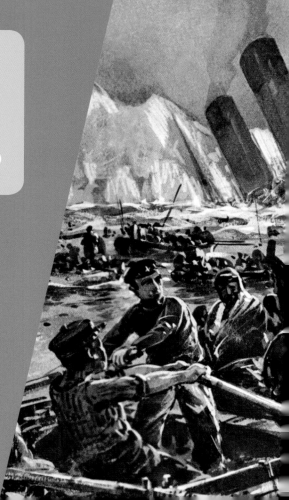

DID YOU KNOW?

The *Titanic* crew called for help. They used **Morse code**. A nearby ship got the message. It sped to the scene. It rescued about 705 survivors.

SOS ● ● ● ▬ ▬ ▬ ● ● ●

stern

CHAPTER 3

LESSONS LEARNED

The sinking of *Titanic* shocked the world. It also led to new laws. *Titanic* did not have enough **lifeboats**. Today, ships need enough lifeboats to fit everybody.

The crew wasn't trained for disasters. Many lifeboats were launched unfilled. Today, both passengers and crew take part in **drills**.

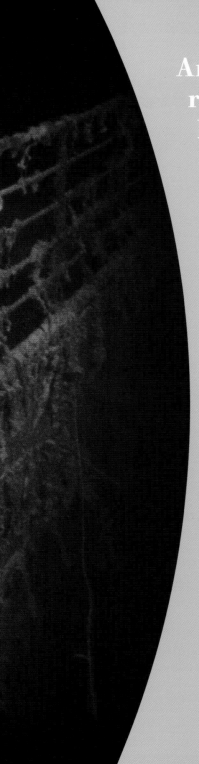

And finally, bulkheads were redesigned. Now they perform better in a disaster. Today's ships may not be unsinkable either. But they are safer.

Titanic rests nearly 2.5 miles (4 kilometers) underwater. It is a museum. It is a graveyard. And after more than 100 years, it still fascinates us.

DID YOU KNOW?

Since it was found in 1985, many explorers have visited the wreck. They have mapped the site. They have taken pictures. And they have found more than 5,500 objects. These include hats, jewelry, and silverware.

ACTIVITIES & TOOLS

MAKE AN ICEBERG

The story of *Titanic* shows how dangerous icebergs can be to ships. In fact, most of the danger lies below the surface of the water. Make your own iceberg and see!

What You Need:
- balloon
- water
- salt
- glass
- plate
- freezer
- clear aquarium or sink
- ruler

❶ Add several tablespoons of salt to a glass of water and stir. Then fill a balloon with the salty water. Tie the end of the balloon.

❷ Place the balloon on a plate and set it in the freezer overnight.

❸ Remove the balloon from the freezer and place it in an aquarium or sink filled with tap water.

❹ The balloon represents an iceberg. Use your ruler to measure how much of the ice is below the water. How much is above? Is the widest point of the iceberg above or below the water line?

GLOSSARY

bow: The forward part of a ship.

bulkheads: Walls used to separate compartments.

crow's nest: A structure on a ship that is used as a lookout point.

drills: Exercises done to teach actions.

elegant: Having qualities of wealth and comfort.

emigrants: People who leave their home countries to make new lives elsewhere.

gash: A long, deep cut.

hull: The sides, bottom, and deck of a ship.

iceberg: A large floating mass of ice detached from a glacier.

lifeboats: Sturdy boats carried by a ship for use in an emergency.

Morse code: A code that uses light or sound in patterns of dots and dashes to represent letters and numbers.

stern: The rear part of a ship.

vessel: A ship or a large boat.

INDEX

bow 16

bulkheads 10, 11, 16, 21

crew 12, 15, 16, 19

crow's nest 5

deaths 16

disaster 7, 19, 21

drills 19

elegant 9

emigrants 12

England 12

gash 15

hull 10, 15

iceberg 5, 15

lifeboats 18, 19

Morse code 16

New York Harbor 12

North Atlantic 5

passengers 4, 12, 15, 19

safest 9, 12, 21

ship 7, 8, 12, 15, 16, 18, 21

stern 16

survivors 16

vessel 7

wealthy 12

TO LEARN MORE

Learning more is as easy as 1, 2, 3.

1) Go to www.factsurfer.com

2) Enter "Titanic" into the search box.

3) Click the "Surf" button to see a list of websites.

With factsurfer, finding more information is just a click away.